MW00979357

Alligator tales

(and crocodiles too!)
For children
(and grown-ups, too)

Miles Smeeton
Illustrated by Eric Grantvedt

Foreword by Clio Smeeton

PELICAN PUBLISHING COMPANY
Gretna 2001

First published under the title *Alligator Tales (and Crocodiles Too!)* by Bayeux Arts, Calgary, Alberta, Canada

Published by arrangement in North America by Pelican Publishing Company, Inc., 2001

First Pelican edition, 2001

The publisher gratefully acknowledges the assistance of the Alberta Foundation for the Arts and the Canada Council.

ISBN: 1-56554-847-7

Printed in Hong Kong
Published by Pelican Publishing Company, Inc.
1000 Burmaster Street, Gretna, Louisiana
70053

To Catriona and Sonamara, for whom these poems were written

ACKNOWLEDGMENTS

STUART AND MARGIE JOHNSTON first took the poems and persuaded their friend Eric Grantvedt to do the illustrations. But then the whole project languished until the untiring efforts of George Parry forced the pictures and the rhymes to the attention of Bob Doull. Bob took the nascent project and involved Bayeux Arts, thus magicking this book into being. I thank them all from the bottom of my heart.

CONTENTS

FOREWORD

ALL HIS LIFE, my father, Miles Smeeton, wrote rhymes on bits of paper about any subject which interested or amused him. His output increased once my children, Catriona and Sonamara, were born and had grown into a conversable age. Children entertained my father. His grandchildren, provided they were polite and interested in the world around them, entertained him even more.

My parents' boat, the boat which I grew up on, was the yacht TZU HANG. She was fitting out for her first successful rounding of Cape Horn, when my eldest daughter, Catriona, was born in South Africa. After Catriona's birth, my parents set off and TZU HANG rounded the Horn in an amazingly fast passage. So fast that, for many years, she held the international record for "Doubling the Horn." The thought of his new, first grandchild prompted my father to send little postcards of poems from every port TZU HANG put into.

By the time Sonamara was born in Spain, TZU HANG was sailing home to Canada via Europe. She put into the same Spanish fjord that we had sailed into when I was eight years old. As though the world had remained unchanged for twenty years the same family, the Boras, were having a summer barbecue. A barbecue of grilled mussels, sardines and red wine, followed by roasted almonds dipped in chocolate. All that they ate was the produce of their own fields and of the mussel bed which filled the fjord in front of their house.

I remembered seeing my first fireflies when I was a child at the Boras' barbecue, running away from the boring rumble of grown-up talk and the leaping flames of the fire into the soft Spanish night. Then the fireflies filled the air, sparkling green in the darkness, in such multitudes that when trapped in a glass bottle they produced light enough to read by.

By the time Sonamara was born, the fireflies had dwindled to an occasional green spark flickering in the hedges. This was just a small indication of what was happening to the natural world, but it was still overwhelming around the excitement of the birth of a new grand child and the start of a new voyage.

For as long as we lived among the green heather-clad fields of Galicia, postcards from my father were carried by the postman to our house in Piedrafita. The postman rode a little gallego pony with his mailbags piled up before the saddle. In the wintertime he would ride up in the blowing snow, wrapped in a poncho and glittering with ice.

The postcards carried the tropics with them. In the rhymes of alligators splashing in tropic streams there were faint reflections of the wake of TZU HANG carrying my parents home to Canada, her sweet eager bow slicing the dark sea. They came home to Alberta, and within a year, we followed them to settle in B.C. But the postcards didn't stop.

Catriona and Sonamara got alligator rhymes as an extra embellishment on their birthdays, for Christmas, or just because my father felt like sending them something. When he wasn't writing books, poems, breaking and backing his horses or working the property, he helped my mother, Beryl, with her swift foxes. Like the vanishing fireflies of Galicia the little swift foxes of the Great Plains had vanished too, but my mother was determined that it should not become a final disappearance for them.

My father never wrote rhymes about the swift foxes for the children. Instead he told them fanciful stories about our neighbour, Mr Fox, and sent them drawings of Mr Fox's barn and fields with Mr Fox in a Stetson lurking behind ramparts of hay and lashing his long bushy tail.

The reintroduction of the swift fox, an animal classified as extinct in Canada and extirpated in over 90 percent of its historic range in the U.S., became central to both my parents' lives. They found the project new, exciting and totally involving. In 1972, when they brought the first swift foxes back to Canada, no other agency, whether government or "green" bureaucracy, showed the slightest interest in what they were doing. Initially, that gave them a free hand. After the animals were declared extinct, and my parents' swift fox breeding program had become a proven success, other agencies became interested in the swift fox reintroduction program.

I have often thought that if one could visualize a small flying carpet, with a little swift fox sitting on it, balancing upon his nose a huge inverted triangle and in that triangle a honeycomb full of people, that would be a visual representation of the swift fox project. Miles' and Beryl's ranch, the only place in the world with a captive breeding colony of swift fox, their success in breeding the foxes and the foxes' proven survival success after release are portrayed by the fox and carpet. Whisk that away, and the triangle and its people crash to the ground.

The Canadian swift fox reintroduction program, which was started by my parents, is close to being the world's first reintroduction of an extirpated carnivore. It is that very rare thing, a happy and nearly successful conservation story. Given the funds to continue three more years, it will be internationally acknowledged to be a complete success. Without funds it will stop and we will see a second extinction of the swift fox in Canada.

Sonamara and Catriona are grown up now and no longer giggling at the supposed antics of Mr Fox. They don't look for postcards from

11

distant shores with exotic stamps and rhymes squeezed in tiny writing on the back, but they do help out with the swift fox reintroduction program. And all the proceeds from the sale of this book will help out with it too.

Clio Smeeton
President, Cochrane Ecological Institute
Cochrane Wildlife Reserve
Cochrane, Alberta, Canada

ALLIGATOR
MEAT

Alligator lightly boiled
Or eaten cold with salad oiled
Is reckoned quite the choicest meat
Like veal and mutton, hard to beat;
Alligator's back is good
When strongly pickled in the wood.
Alligator dried in trees,
Alligator fried in grease—
That tasty alligator.

Not so savoury, I do fear,
is an alligator's ear;
But fricassee of gators' knees
With parmesan and sweet green peas
Is something one must munch
When famous people come to lunch.
Alligator, so they say,
Is a dish that saves the day—
Plain soft-boiled alligator.

Alligator is excellent food
Provided you are in the mood.
"Tis better far that you should eat
Than be an alligator's treat
Or, an alfresco dish
Always eaten after fish.
I do like gator, but still I say
I would prefer to end the day—
Outside an alligator.

THE
OCEAN-GOING
CROCODILE

From Timor to the Torres Strait
From Arnhem Bay to Yapero,
I sail the Arafura Sea
And all the ships give way to me!
So drop your sail and wait a while
Let pass the ocean crocodile.
Avast there, away, and yo ho hay.

The currents of Endeavour Strait
Or in the Halmahera Sea
Are quite unable to prevail
Against the power of my tail!
Though high aloft your canvas pile,
You cannot beat the crocodile.
Avast there, give way, and yo ho hay.

When half-submerged, I take my ease
And scan the sky as I do please;
I often hear a captain call,
"The crocodile! Now stand by all
And dip the flag in proud salute
Towards that ocean-going brute"
Avast there, belay, and yo ho hay.

Honour me then as I should be
Honoured by those who ply the sea,
But should a sailor once revile
The ocean-going crocodile,
He'd find himself in sudden grief
Upon a far, uncharted reef.
Avast there, hurray, and yo ho hay.

When, as the shadows dull the waves
And hoary spume fills up the air,
The lookout high upon the mast
May see the ocean croc go fast;
Let fly your sheet and helpless stand:
Here comes the beast from Arnhem Land!
Avast there, away, and yo ho hay.

YACHTING
ALLIGATORS

Two alligators in a boat
Set out to sail the sea
Though both could swim
And both could float
As easy as could be.
They chose instead to sit at ease
And speak of what is new,
While peeling spuds and shelling peas
For Alligator Stew.

They sailed beyond the river's mouth
Upon the Indies Ocean
And while they thought the view was fine
They didn't like the motion.
So they put about and spent the day
East of Dondra Head,
Discussing stew that they would brew
Before they went to bed.

"A little rice, a pinch of thyme,
A splendid stew we'll fix.
Look in the locker down below
For Alligator Mix.

"Synthetic powder" reads the can,
"made from protein gators need,
From flesh of dog and barking deer
With fetid flavour guaranteed."

The sun it set, and the gentle scent
Of flowers renewed by dew
Came out to join the foul ferment
Of Alligator Stew.
The moon she rose across the sky,
A steady course she kept,
To rumbling gurgitations while
The alligators slept.

ALLIGATOR
AIR CREW

Alligator flying high
Sun-bright clouds below,
Vapour trails across the sky,
Who on earth would know?
Quite relaxed upon your seat
You're served by alligatress neat;
Planes indeed are very few
That have an alligator crew.

The pilot who is in control
Has an alligator smile.
The steward in quite another role
Is, alas, a crocodile;
But on this plane there must not be
Species prejudice, don't you see;
And far the happiest of them all
Is the stewardess Ghariyal.*

* A fish-eating crocodile from India.

Her uniform is dashing green
And mottled brown with patches
And after takeoff she's soon seen
Displaying all the hatches
And how to latch your seatbelt
In a toothy way most charming,
And telling how you may escape
Without being too alarming.

When Ghariyal walks down the aisle
Offering peanuts and hot drinks
Flashing her razor-sharpened smile,
A storm of happy nods and winks
Follow in her path. You'd never guess,
Despite her friendliness
That all the alligator crew
Has rather different tastes than you.

PS: Nor of the secret understanding
They have about you, after landing.

ALLIGATOR
IN A BALLOON

Alligator in a balloon,
Don't come down too
soon, too soon.
Sailing so high in the tranquil air,
Tell me what do you see and where?
Mountains shimmering far away?
Rippling streams where you'd like to play?
Alligator, stay right there,
While earthbound mortals stop and stare
To see you fly.

Alligator in a balloon
Cousin of the moon, the moon,
Up in the sky there is no wrong
Far away from the scurrying throng;
High aloft the air is clean,
You travel along where you've never been,
Above a barn and a grazing cow;
Alligator, don't come down now
But by and by.

Alligator in a balloon,
Can you wait till the afternoon?
When you're wondering what's to eat
Thinking of some juicy meat;
When both the fuel and lift have gone
And there's some place soft to land upon,
It best be near a murmuring stream
Where you may bathe and sleep and dream
Of your day on high.

ALLIGATOR
TEARS

In an alligator's dream
Gently musing,
Below the surface of the stream
Softly cruising,
With the silence of its banks
And its waving weedy ranks,
There's always something good to eat:
A juicy steak of fresh raw meat,
Rich and oozing.

In an alligator's eyes
Calmly lazing,
You will see a strange surmise
While he's gazing,
Wondering if you will provide
A stomach ache when you're inside
Or, if eaten on the bank,
Your flavour sweet or rank
He'll be praising.

In an alligator's tears,
Wetly crying,
You might see confirmed the fears
That send you flying
From suspicion of a threat
That perhaps he'll get you yet;
But rest assured that he would weep
As he planned his fateful leap,
Softly sighing.

BATHROOM ALLIGATOR

Slimy alligator, I hate to touch you
And you know why.
Alligator, go and dry.
And don't leave footsteps in the hall
But rather leave no marks at all
Along your path.
Alligator, given rope,
I know that you would leave the soap
Upon the floor,
And what is more
You'd leave the water in the bath.

Please pull the plug.
And, Alligator, brush your teeth,
Those fangs projecting underneath
That knobbly nose will soon decay
If you don't clean them every day.
Pick up the mat
And hang it on the rail,
So, Alligator, mind your tail
Is tucked in bed;

Then, Alligator, rest your head
On clean white sheets
And if everything meets
With my approval, perhaps I might
Kiss you a fond good night,
Good night.

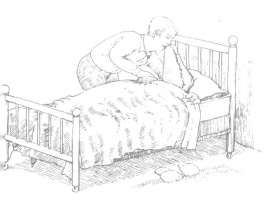

FOUR LITTLE ALLIGATORS

Four little alligators walking went
Along the shadowed river bank
And all of them thought the time well spent
As horny feet in the sedge grass sank—
For an alligator truly knows
The pleasure of mud between the toes,
Of mud between the toes.

They swam upriver amongst the reeds;
Four little alligators all well fed;
They searched for a place an alligator needs
Where ripples talk on a pebbly bed—
For an alligator truly knows
The pleasure of ripples between the toes,
Of rippling water between the toes.

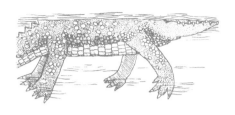

Then four little alligators drifted home
On sun-dappled waves beneath the trees;
Though alligators love to roam,
This they like best: to drift at ease—
For an alligator knows
The pleasure of rest while the river flows,
And tickles them gently between the toes.

THE
YELLOW-BELLIED
ALLIGATOR

A yellow-bellied alligator
Is a sight most rare;
According to existing data
There now exists a pair
In the Hullabaloo Mountains
In the Hullabaloo Range,
Playing in the fountains
In a way most strange.

Many scientists come a-walking,
Bearded, booted and bespecked,
Packs on backs and wisely talking,
Alligators to inspect.
In the Hullabaloo Valleys,
In the Hullabaloo Hills,
Scientists are making sallies,
Mountain-sick and popping pills.

When the north wind blows a freezer
Then the alligator pair
Ride the Hullabaloo Geyser
And soak in hot pools there.
That, the scientists tell us,
Is the reason for their plight;
It's hot water that turns their bellies
Into such an ugly sight.

SIREN
ALLIGATOR

Once in a blue moon, Alligator,
You are said to sing
A song of such exquisite beauty
Like faerie bells that ring,
Calling men from duty,
Stumbling mesmerized,
Splashing through march and mangrove
Only to be surprised
At the hideous throat that calls them
And totally enthralls them
When the moon is blue.

Once in a blue moon, Alligator,
You raise that lovely voice
And have the power of calling
Men with no other choice
But to hasten, wading falling,
Exhausted, crippled, dazed,
Brother turned 'gainst brother
In disbelief amazed
At the glorious voice that hauls them
To a mouth that so appalls them
When the moon is blue.

Once in a blue moon, Alligator,
And that be praised, is rare,
Men hear your wanton fluting
So wild and strange an air
The countryside polluting
Though magically conceived,
A dirge, a devil's pibroch

For those to be
bereaved
As you start the
swampland ringing
Sad victims to you
bringing
When the moon is
blue.

TEMPLE
ALLIGATOR

Sardonic alligator
Whose smile is so deceiving,
Keeper of the devil's mews
In all ill believing,
Sampler of rotten meat,
Aged awkward and effete,
Nothing good achieving.

What's behind this sultry leer
On the warm stone lying?
Perverted ESP, I fear,
Into secrets prying,
Knowing you will long outlive
Humble men who pray and give
Flowers, "Ram Ram" crying.

Age perhaps has made you wise,
Those scaly lids concealing
Frightful alligator eyes,
All fearas, all hopes revealing.
No wonder Life's open book
Gives you that weird, demonic look
Of crafty double-dealing.

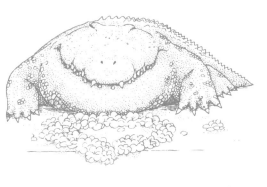

ALLIGATOR'S BATTLE SONG

Alligators courageous,
Let us sing a song
Of spurious adventure
And errant righting wrong,
Of how we caught an Abbot
Washing in a brook
And quickly pulled him under
Despite his Holy Book.

Alligators courageous,
Sing how we won the war
That chased our crocodile foe
Beyond our farthest roar.
Sing how we deftly drew a line
On the map of worldly powers
That led the U.N. to define
That all this side is ours.

Alligators courageous,
Dancing in the glen,
Rings on scaly fingers
Snatch'd from bathing men.
Let the welkin thunder
With our martial tread,
Welcome those who blunder
Upon our watery bed.

Alligators courageous,
Secret killers all,
Masters of the ambush,
The underwater brawl.
Weave the laurel wreath then
'Round the horny head
For inhumanity is in
And innocence is dead.